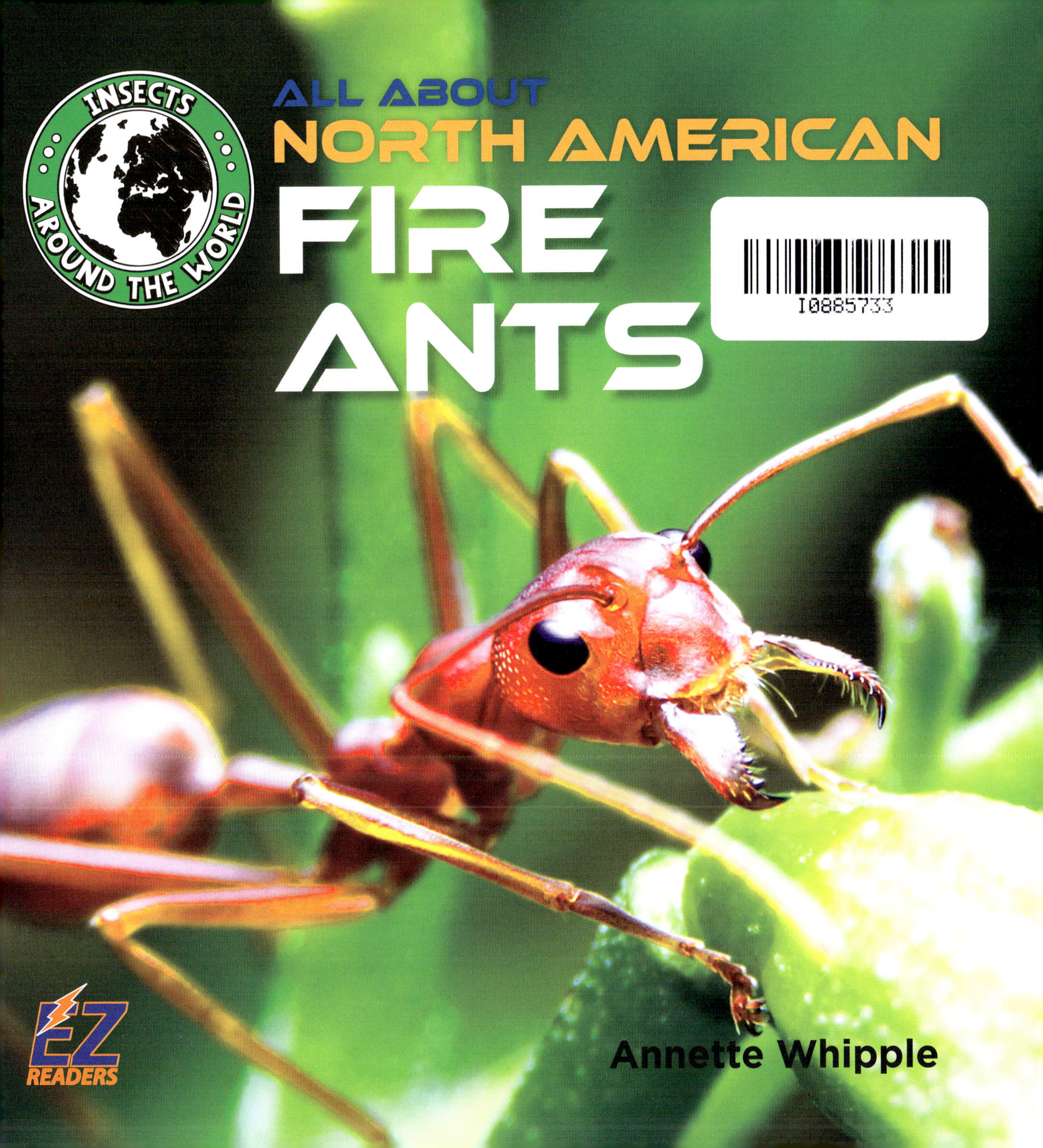

INSECTS AROUND THE WORLD

ALL ABOUT NORTH AMERICAN FIRE ANTS

Annette Whipple

EZ READERS

Creating Young Nonfiction Readers

EZ Readers lets children delve into nonfiction at beginning reading levels. Young readers are introduced to new concepts, facts, ideas, and vocabulary.

Tips for Reading Nonfiction with Beginning Readers

Talk about Nonfiction

Begin by explaining that nonfiction books give us information that is true. The book will be organized around a specific topic or idea, and we may learn new facts through reading.

Look at the Parts

Most nonfiction books have helpful features. Our *EZ Readers* include color photographs and graphic aids, a table of contents, a glossary, and an index. Share the purpose of these features with your reader.

Color Photos and Graphic Aids
A lot of information can be found by "reading" photos, charts, maps, and other graphic aids found within nonfiction texts. Help your reader learn more about the different ways information can be displayed.

Table of Contents
Located at the front of the book, this list shows the big ideas within the text and the page numbers where they can be found.

Glossary
Located at the back of the book, the glossary defines key words and phrases that are related to the topic. These words and phrases can be found in the text in colored type.

Index
Located at the back of the book, an index is an alphabetical list of topics and the page numbers where they can be found.

With a little help and guidance about reading nonfiction, you can feel good about introducing a young reader to the world of *EZ Readers* nonfiction books.

Mitchell Lane
PUBLISHERS

2001 SW 31st Avenue
Hallandale, FL 33009
www.mitchelllane.com

First Edition, 2025.

Author: Annette Whipple
Designer: Rhea Magaro
Editor: Kim Thompson

Names/credits:
Title: All About North American Fire Ants / by Annette Whipple
Description: Hallandale, FL :
Mitchell Lane Publishers, [2025]

Series: Insects Around the World
Library bound ISBN: 978-1-68020-954-9
eBook ISBN: 978-1-68020-961-7

EZ Readers is an imprint of
Mitchell Lane Publishers

PHOTO CREDITS
Alamy: B.A.E. Inc., 12-13; Vinícius Souza, 16-17; iStock: vnarong, cover, 1; Hakase_, 18-19; Shutterstock: ChaiyaTN, 4-5; Lamyai, 6-7; Wayne Broussard, 8-9; PUMPZA, 10-11; Piyapong pc, 14-15; Yuttana Joe, 20-21

Paperback ISBN: 979-8-89260-142-9

CONTENTS

Fire ants can be as small as the tip of a sharp crayon or as big as a grain of rice. Once, these **insects** only lived on the continent of South America. But they crawled on ships and came to North America.

Fire ants get their name from their painful stings, which contain **venom**. Their stings feel like a nasty burn. Fire ants sting to protect against spiders and other **predators**. They also sting people.

Fire ants live in forests, deserts, and grasslands. If there is water, they like to stay near it. Fire ants hold on to each other when water floods. They float together like a raft.

Fire ants live in groups called **colonies**. They make mounds from soil and live inside. Some colonies have just one queen that lays eggs. Others have many queens.

Most of the time, fire ants stay inside their mound. On warm days, some fire ants use underground tunnels to leave the colony. They go out to look for food.

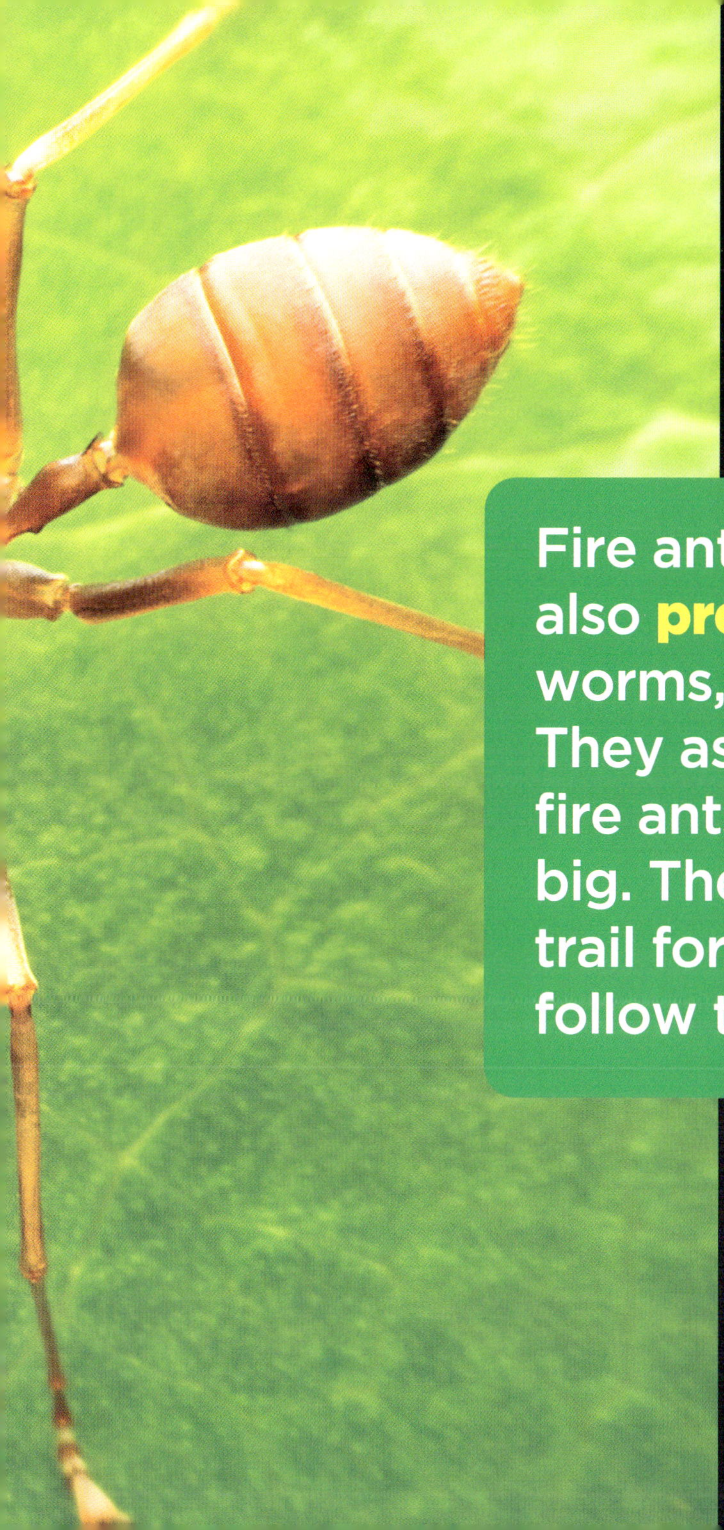

Fire ants eat plants. They also **prey** on other insects, worms, birds, and mammals. They ask for help from other fire ants when food is too big. They leave a **chemical** trail for other fire ants to follow to the food.

Queen fire ants have wings. Males also have wings. They fly in the air to mate. Each queen wants to start a new colony. She might first lay 10 to 15 eggs in the spring. Then she lays more. In a few years, there can be more than 100,000 fire ants in a colony.

Fire ants do more harm than good. Their stings hurt people. They damage **crops**. They kill farm animals and wild animals. They can even eat through power lines.

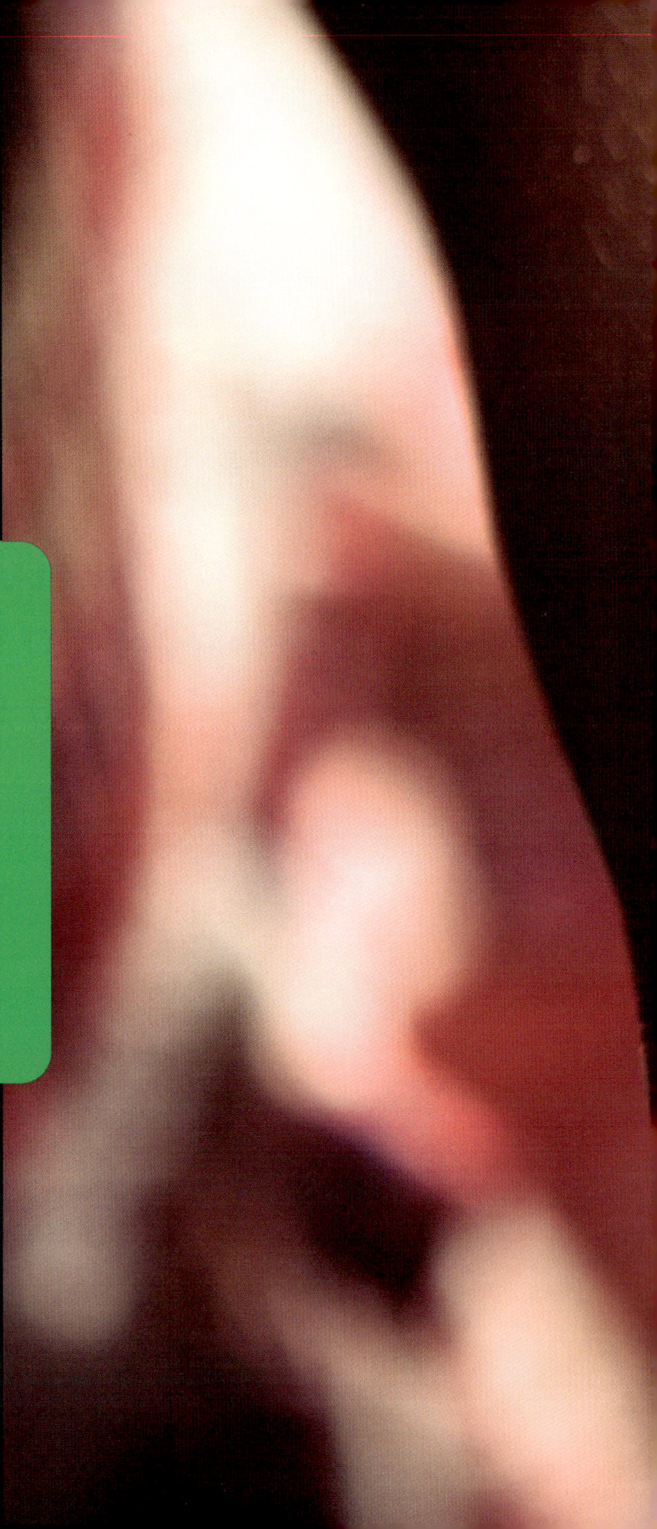

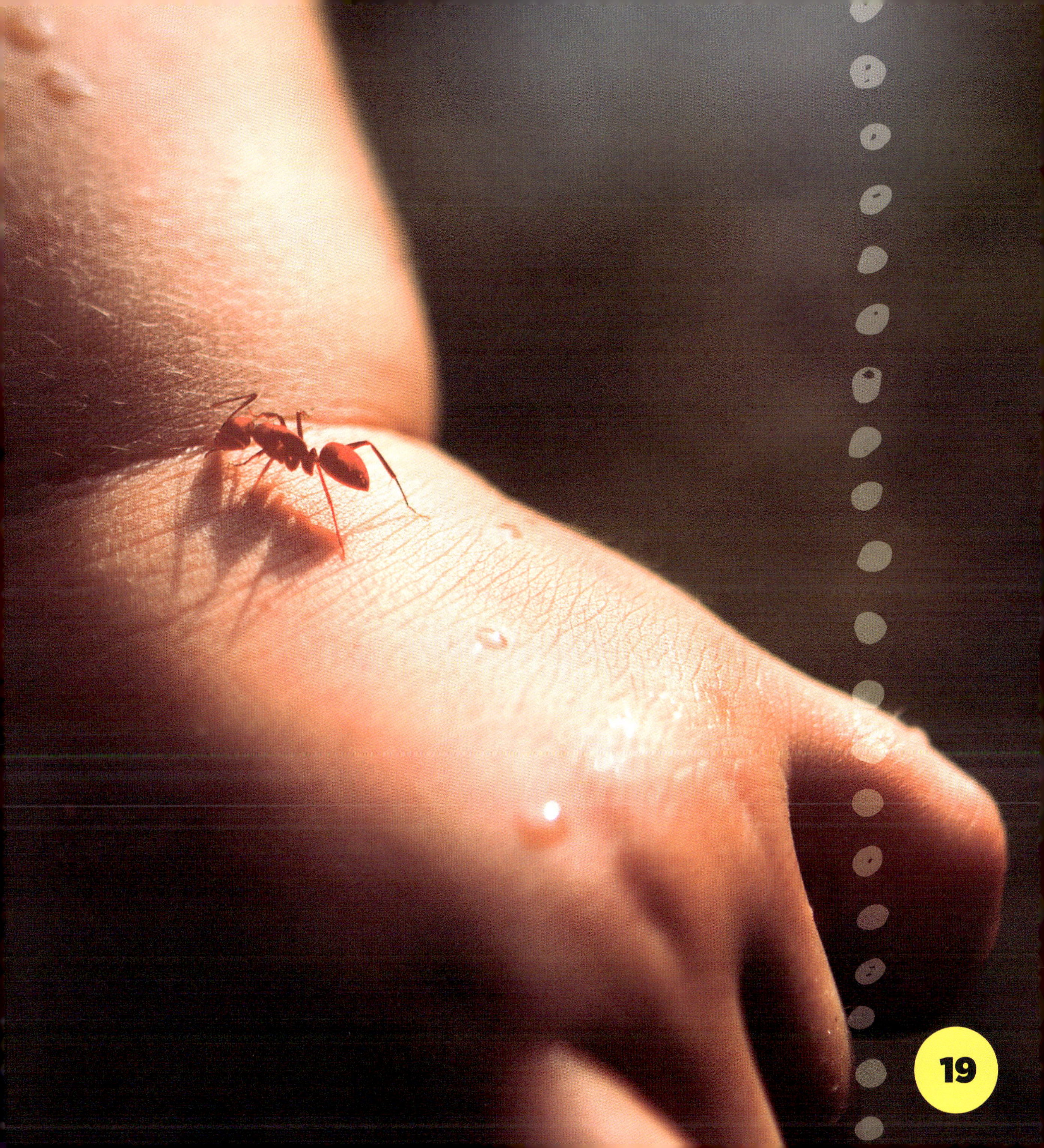

But fire ants can also be helpful. They kill many **pests**. They eat fleas, ticks, cockroach eggs, and more. The tunnels they build in soil help plants get air and water.

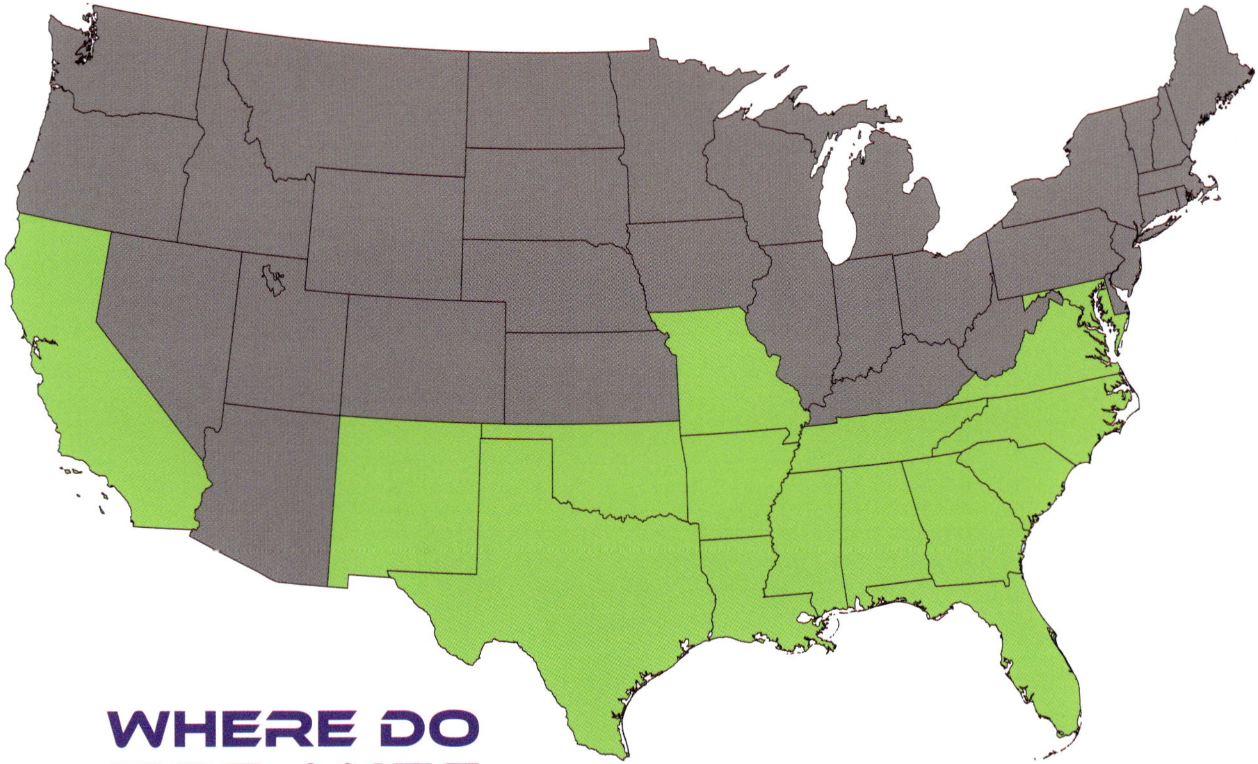

WHERE DO FIRE ANTS LIVE?

About 100 years ago, fire ants hitched a ride on ships coming from South America. Now, they live in the southern United States. They can be found as far west as California and as far north as Virginia in a variety of habitats.

INTERESTING FACTS

- Fire ants can survive both floods and droughts.
- Fire ants kill many birds that nest on the ground.
- Tunnel exits can be 25 feet (eight meters) from a fire ant mound.
- Fire ant stings can be life-threatening for some people.
- Female fire ants are red, and males are black.

PARTS OF A FIRE ANT

Legs
The back legs of fire ants are longer than the middle and front legs.

Mandibles
Fire ants hold on to prey with strong jaws called mandibles. Then, they sting!

Spiracles
Instead of lungs, fire ants breathe through holes in their bodies called spiracles.

Stinger
Fire ants use their stingers to put venom into their predators and their prey.

Wings
Females who can become queens and all male fire ants have wings.

GLOSSARY

chemical (KEM-i-kuhl)
A substance that is found in nature or that is made by living things and that may be detected by other living things

colonies (KAH-luh-neez)
Large groups of animals that live together

crops (krahps)
Plants that farmers grow as food for people or animals

insects (IN-sekts)
Small animals with hard outer skeletons, six legs, and three body sections

pests (pests)
Insects or other animals that cause destruction and damage, especially on farms

predators (PRED-uh-turz)
Animals that hunt and eat other animals

prey (pray)
To hunt an animal for food

venom (VEN-uhm)
Poison that is produced by some animals and delivered through a bite or sting

INDEX

FURTHER READING

McDonald, Jill. *Exploring Insects*. New York, NY: Doubleday, 2023.

McKay, Chason. *How Do Ants Survive a Flood?* Franklin, TN: Flowerpot Press, 2022.

ON THE INTERNET

Entomology Animated: Fire Ant Venom
https://www.youtube.com/watch?v=0991pAmvdLo
Learn all about the science behind fire ant venom.

National Institute of Environmental Health Sciences: Fire Ants and Asian Needle Ants
https://kids.niehs.nih.gov/topics/natural-world/wildlife/insects/ants
Learn how fire ants came to North America and more.